INST/

FRENCH

by Dorothy and David Thomas

Editorial Consultant:
Jean-Marc Capello

Illustrated by DRAGONFLY DESIGNS

dot publications

New edition 1990
Copyright © D. M.. & D.W. S. Thomas 1988, 1990

_____

Published by dot Publications
School House, Glendinning Terrace, Galashiels TD1 2JW

_____

ISBN 1 8710 8600 0

Printed by Charter Press Ltd., Rhuddlan, N. Wales

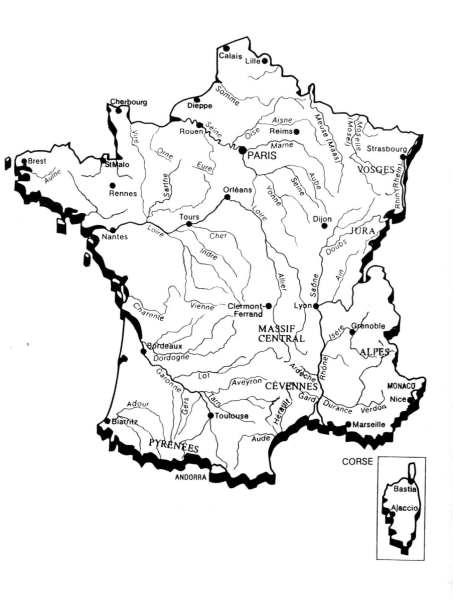

Contents

Introduction

If you've never spoken a word of a foreign language before, or you've forgotten everything you learned at school, your problems are now over.

With DoT Publications' *Instant* phrasebooks you can find what you need fast. Just read the speech bubbles off the page.

First we help you pronounce it right with the easy guide on page 7. As well as the pronunciation, we show you where to put the emphasis by setting the right word or part of a word in **heavy** type.

Next we take you through a series of typical tourist situations, giving you the words to say to get what you want, followed by some idea of the replies you are likely to hear. In most cases we give you a basic situation which can be used in lots of places – for example, the phrases used in the baker's shop dialogue on page 24 can be used to buy things in most other kinds of shop too.

Finally, at the back you'll find a short section explaining the most important points of French grammar. Right at the back is a list of numbers. Learn these first if you can – numbers are a vital part of any language and will make talking to people very much easier.

Remember, travel abroad should be fun, and making your way in the local language is a big part of it. We hope to help you enjoy yourself on your trip.

Bon voyage!

French Sounds

We have tried to keep our pronunciation system as simple as possible so that you can read the questions and answers in each picture almost as if they were English.

If you are not sure what a particular word should sound like, check it with this guide to individual sounds:

a or **a–** is always short, as in **m**at.
ah is long, as in **fa**ther, **Sha**h.
ahr: say **are** then widen your mouth – **aaa**rh!
ay is like **a** in l**a**te.

e is always short as in m**e**t.
er is like **ur** in f**ur**, but the **r** is barely pronounced.
o is short as in h**o**t (but it is pronounced **oh** at end of words).
oh is like **o** in n**o**te.
r is rolled at the back of the throat.
s is always pronounced like **s** in **s**ee.

uh is like **u** in b**u**n or **uh** in H**uh**!
ur is like **ur** in f**ur**, but the **r** is barely pronounced.
uw is like nothing in English: purse your lips quite tightly as if you are going to whistle, then say it as it looks.
y is pronounced **ee** or like **y** in **y**ou (never like **y** in nyl**o**n).
zh is like **s** in mea**s**ure.

Nasal vowels
ang, ong: try holding the end of your nose (only when practising!). Don't stress the **g**, it should barely be there.

Vowels
English vowels are often diphthongs (more than one sound, e.g. sh**ow**). French vowels never change the sound in the middle.

Stress
English tends to stress the most important words in each sentence. French sentences, however, have a regular rhythm, so that the stress usually falls on the last syllable of a sentence or group or words.

Any letters printed in **heavy** type should be stressed. If a word has no **heavy** letters it should be pronounced as evenly as possible.

Hotels

France has lots of hotels. Prices are quoted per room, not per person, and breakfast is usually an optional extra. You will often be invited to inspect a room before taking it. If you would prefer a bigger, smaller or quieter one, say so — no one will mind.

1. **Bongzhoor,** ma-**dam.** Zhay rayz**air**vay uwn shahmbr poor suh swahr.

3. Oh nom duh Jones.

If you've booked

2. Wee, mu**syuh.** Say a kell nom?

4. Byang onton**duw.** Say la shahmbr **nuw**mayroh deece. Votr passpor, seelvoo**play.**

1. *Bonjour, madame. J'ai réservé une chambre pour ce soir.*
   Good day. I have booked a room for tonight.

3. *Au nom de Jones.*
   My name is Jones.

2. *Oui, monsieur. C'est à quel nom?*
   Yes sir, what name is it?

4. *Bien entendu. C'est la chambre numéro dix (10). Votre passeport, s'il vous plaît.*
   Of course. It's room no. 10.
   May I have your passport, please?

---

chambre avec
petit déjeuner
room with breakfast

demi-pension   *pension complète*
half-board   full board

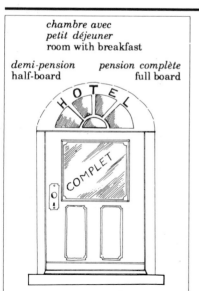

Prefer something less exotic? This means "Bed and breakfast".

CHAMBRE D'HÔTE

If you *haven't* booked, and you find this sign on the door, or if the receptionist says "Say complay" *(c'est complet)*, it's full. If you *have* booked, go on in anyway. If not, try another hotel and turn the page.

In larger towns, the Tourist Information Office will fix a hotel booking for you (many speak English). Look out for *Syndicat d'Initiative, Office de Tourisme* or the sign:

*Ignore signs for *Hôtel de Ville* and *Hôtel-Dieu* if you're just in search of a bed for the night – the first means Town Hall, and the second is the hospital.

1. *Bonjour, monsieur. Je voudrais une chambre pour ce soir.*
   Good day. I'd like a room for tonight.

2. *Oui, monsieur. Pour combien de personnes?*
   Certainly. For how many people?

3. *Pour deux personnes (et deux enfants).*
   For two people (and two children).

4. *Bien. C'est pour combien de nuits, monsieur?*
   Fine. For how many nights, sir?

5. *Pour une nuit.*
   For one night.

1. *Est-ce que vous désirez un grand lit ou des lits jumeaux?*
   Would you like a double bed or twin beds?

2. *Des lits jumeaux, s'il vous plaît.*
   Twin beds, please.

3. *Avec bain, douche, toilettes?*
   With bath, shower, toilet?

4. *Avec douche et toilettes.*
   With shower and toilet.

9

Booking a Hotel Room

1. *Nous avons une chambre au premier étage. C'est la chambre numéro dix-huit (18).*
   We have a room on the first floor. It's number 18.

3. *Le prix de la chambre est de deux cent (200) francs.*
   The room costs 200 francs.

2. *Bien. C'est combien?*
   Good. How much is it?

4. *Très bien. Nous la prenons.*
   Fine. We'll take it.

la klay
la clef
the key

1. *Bien. Votre nom, s'il vous plaît, et votre passeport.*
   Good. Your name please, and your passport.

3. *Voulez-vous signer ici.*
   Please sign here.

5. *Merci. Voici la clef de votre chambre.*
   Thank you. Here is the key to your room.

2. *Voilà. Je m'appelle Baker.*
   There you are. My name is Baker.

4. *Merci.*
   Thank you.

lay bag**gazh**
les bagages
the luggage

10

Inspecting the room

1. Pweezh vwahr la shahmor?
2. Byang suwr, musyuh.
3. *(If you like it)* Bong, noo la prunnong.

OR

(If you don't) Nong, ell ay troh brweeyont (puh-teet). Avvay voo kellkuh shoze duh mee-ur?

4. Zhuh swee dayzolay, musyuh ...

1. *Puis-je voir la chambre?*
   May I see the room?
2. *Bien sûr, monsieur.*
   Of course, sir.

3. *Bon, nous la prenons.*
   Good, we'll take it.

OR

Non, elle est trop bruyante (petite). Avez-vous quelque chose de mieux?
   No, it's too noisy (small). Have you anything better?

4. *Je suis désolé, monsieur ...*
   I'm sorry sir ...

Meals at the hotel

1. A kell ur sairvay voo luh deenay? (puh-tee dayzhurnay/dayzhurnay)
2. A set ur ay duh-mee.

1. *A quelle heure servez-vous le dîner? (petit déjeuner / déjeuner)*
   What time do you serve dinner? (breakfast/lunch)
2. *A sept heures et demie.*
   At 7.30.

(Time p.72)

Checking out

1. Voolay voo muh prayparray la not seelvooplay?
2. Oh vwahr.

1. *Voulez-vous me préparer la note, s'il vous plaît?*
   Please may I have the bill?
2. *Au revoir.*
   Goodbye.

(Methods of payment p.32)

11

Self-catering

Finding your Gîte
You will generally know the name of your landlord or landlady, so just ask:

1. Oo ab**beet** ma-**dam** –? OR 2. Zhuh shairsh mu**syuh** –.

1. *Où habite Madame –?*
   Where does Mrs. – live?

2. *Je cherche Monsieur –.*
   I'm looking for Mr. –.

The kitchen – La cuisine
La Kwee**zeen**

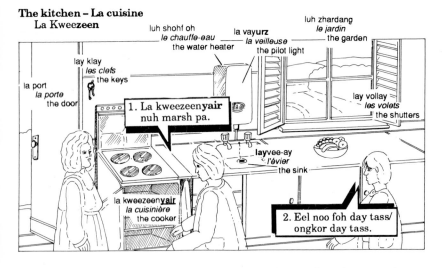

luh shohf oh
le chauffe-eau
the water heater

la va**yurz**
la veilleuse
the pilot light

luh zhardang
le jardin
the garden

lay klay
les clefs
the keys

la port
la porte
the door

lay vollay
les volets
the shutters

1. La kweezeen**yair** nuh marsh pa.

layvee-ay
l'évier
the sink

la kweezeen**yair**
la cuisinière
the cooker

2. Eel noo foh day tass/ ongkor day tass.

1. *La cuisinière ne marche pas.*
   The cooker isn't working.

2. *Il nous faut des tasses / encore des tasses.*
   We need some cups/ some more cups.

12

At the gîte – *A la gîte* – Alla zheet

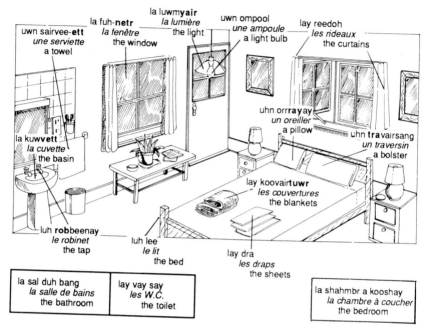

la luwmyair
la lumière
the light

uwn sairvee-**ett**
une serviette
a towel

la fuh-**netr**
la fenêtre
the window

uwn ompool
une ampoule
a light bulb

lay reedoh
les rideaux
the curtains

la kuwv**ett**
la cuvette
the basin

uhn orr**ray**ay
un oreiller
a pillow

uhn tr**a**vairsang
un traversin
a bolster

luh **robb**eenay
le robinet
the tap

luh lee
le lit
the bed

lay koovair**tuwr**
les couvertures
the blankets

lay dra
les draps
the sheets

la sal duh bang	lay vay say
la salle de bains	*les W.C.*
the bathroom	the toilet

la shahmbr a kooshay
la chambre à coucher
the bedroom

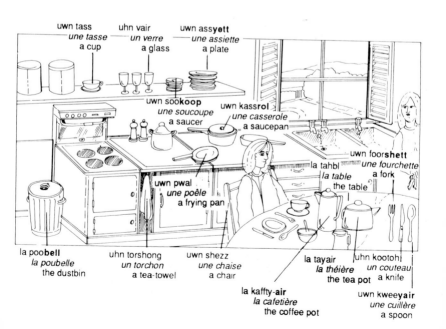

uwn tass
une tasse
a cup

uhn vair
un verre
a glass

uwn ass**yett**
une assiette
a plate

uwn soo**koop**
une soucoupe
a saucer

uwn kass**rol**
une casserole
a saucepan

uwn foor**shett**
une fourchette
a fork

la tahbl
la table
the table

uwn pwal
une poêle
a frying pan

la poo**bell**
la poubelle
the dustbin

uhn torshong
un torchon
a tea-towel

uwn shezz
une chaise
a chair

la tayair
la théière
the tea pot

uhn kootoh
un couteau
a knife

la kaffty-**air**
la cafetière
the coffee pot

uwn kwee**yair**
une cuillère
a spoon

13

Camping

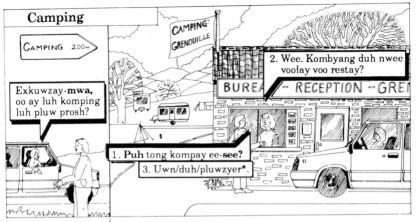

Excusez-moi, où est le camping le plus proche?

Excuse me, where is the nearest campsite?

1. *Peut-on camper ici?*
   May we camp here?

3. *Une / deux / plusieurs**
   One/two/several*

2. *Oui. Combien de nuits voulez-vous rester?*
   Yes. How many nights do you want to stay?

Campsite signs	
EAU POTABLE	Drinking water
No washing	DEFENSE DE LAVER
LAVABOS	Wash basins
DAMES	HOMMES
Women	Men
VAISSELLE	Washing-up
POUBELLES	ORDURES
Dustbins	Rubbish
VIDOIR DE W.C CHIMIQUES	Chemical Toilet Disposal Point

1. *Vous êtes combien de personnes?*
   How many are there of you?

3. *Nous avons une voiture et une tente / caravane / camping-car.*
   We have a car and a tent/caravan/motor caravan.

2. *Deux adultes et un / deux / trois* enfants.*
   Two adults and one/two/three* children.

(*See note about numbers on page 80)

14

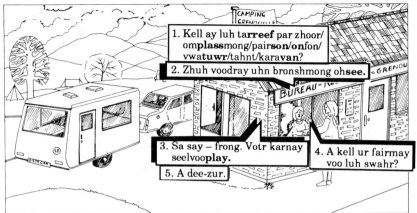

1. *Quel est le tarif par jour /
   emplacement / personne / enfant /
   voiture / tente / caravane?*

   How much does it cost per
   day/pitch/person/child/car/
   tent/caravan?

3. *Ça c'est – francs. Votre carnet,
   s'il vous plaît.*

   That will be – francs. Your
   carnet, please.

2. *Je voudrais un branchement
   aussi.*

   I'd like a power hook-up too.

4. *A quelle heure fermez-vous le
   soir?*

   What time do you close in
   the evening?

5. *A dix heures.*
   At 10 o'clock.

International Camping Carnet

Widely accepted at campsites overseas as
an identity document. Although it is sel-
dom obligatory, it is useful not to have to
leave your passport in reception – you'll
need it for other things like changing
money at the bank, after all.

The Youth Hostel

L'Auberge de jeunesse
(Oh**bairzh** duh zhur**ness**)

Père aubergiste = Warden (pair ohbair-zheest)

1. *Bonsoir. Avez-vous des lits pour ce soir?*
   Good evening. Have you any beds for
   tonight?

3. *Oui, il y a un lit au dortoir numéro
   quatre.*
   Yes, there is a bed in dormitory no. 4.

2. *Voici ma carte d'adhérent.*
   Here's my
   membership card.

4. *Avez-vous un sac à
   viande?*
   Have you a sheet
   sleeping bag?

Eating out

There's a lot of choice when eating out in France, but not everywhere does everything. Broadly speaking, things divide up like this:

un! bar — coffee and drinks, sometimes snacks
un café — breakfast, coffee, drinks and snacks
un cafétéria / libre-service / self — self-service cafeteria
une crêperie — sweet and savoury pancakes
   (crêpes / krepp — *galettes* / gal-**let**)
une brasserie — large café serving quick hot meals
un restaurant — wide variety of meals and prices
une auberge / un relais — country inn serving meals
un relais routier — roadside restaurant for long-distance travellers
grillades — grills; *friterie* — fried food

The MENU as understood by an English-speaker is *La Carte*. Most restaurants have several set meals *(menus)* at fixed prices. *"Je prends le menu à cent francs"* (Zhuh prahn luh muh-**nuw** a song frong) means "I'd like the 100-franc menu". Within each set menu there is often a choice, sometimes at extra charge *(en supplément)*. Dishes on the *à la carte* menu are priced individually and work out more expensive for a full meal.

les plats du jour — the day's special dishes
   (plats à emporter — take-away food)
garni — served with vegetables
maison — home-made or house speciality
du pays — local produce
boisson (non) comprise — wine, beer/mineral water (not) included
service (non) compris — service (not) included

You will often be asked: *Vous avez choisi?*
(voo**zavv**ay shwa**zz**ee) — Have you decided (chosen)? and
Vous avez terminé? (voo**zavv**ay **tair**meenay) — Have you finished?

N.B. Be prepared to hold on to your knife and fork if having several savoury courses.

Meals

le petit déjeuner (luh puh-tee **dayz**hurnay) — continental breakfast
le déjeuner (luh **dayz**hurnay) — lunch, served 12.00-14.00
le dîner (luh **dee**nay) — dinner, served from about 19.30

Cafés usually serve snacks as well as both alcoholic and soft drinks, and of course, coffee. It is cheaper to drink at the bar, but you should not order and pay there and then sit at a table.

A votr sontay!   Bon appay**tee**!
   À votre santé!   *Bon appétit!*
     Cheers!   Enjoy your meal!

Ordering drinks and snacks

krock mus**yuh**
croque-monsieur
toasted cheese
and ham sandwich

uwn beey**air** press**yong**
une bière pression
a draught beer

uwn beey**air**
une bière
bottled beer

uhn zhuw dor**onzh**
un jus d'orange
an orange juice

freet
frites/friterie
chips

1. Zhuh voodray vwahr la kart, seelvoo**play**.

2. Zhuh voodray uhn kaffay, uwn pressyong ay uhn seetrong pressay.

3. Kesskuh voozavvay kom son**veech**?

4. Noo**zav**vong day son**veech** oh zhombong ay oh frommazh.

5. Al-**lor**, duh son**veech** oh frommazh ay duh oh zhombong.

1. *Je voudrais voir la carte, s'il vous plaît.*
   Please could I have the menu.

2. *Je voudrais un café, une pression et un citron pressé.*
   I'd like a black coffee, a (draught) beer and a lemon juice.

3. *Qu'est-ce que vous avez comme sandwichs?*
   What sandwiches have you got?

4. *Nous avons des sandwichs au jambon et au fromage.*
   We have ham and cheese sandwiches.

5. *Alors, deux sandwichs au fromage et deux au jambon.*
   Two cheese sandwiches and two ham, then.

Set plass, ett-ell **okk**uwpay?

Cette place, est-elle occupée?
Is this seat taken?

Paying, finding the W.C.

SNACKS AT ANY TIME

CASSE CROÛTE à toute heure

TOILETTES

1. Pardong, oo song lay twa-**lett**?

2. Lad**dees**yong, seelvoo**play**.

1. *Pardon, où sont les toilettes?*
   Excuse me, where are the toilets?

2. *L'addition, s'il vous plaît.*
   May I have the bill, please.

Breakfast

1. *Monsieur! (or Madame or Mademoiselle)* Waiter/waitress.

2. *Vous désirez, messieurs / dames?* What would you like?

3. *Nous voulons prendre le petit déjeuner complet.* We would like a full breakfast.

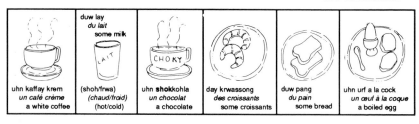

duw lay *du lait* some milk		uhn **shok**kohla *un chocolat* a chocolate	day krwassong *des croissants* some croissants	duw pang *du pain* some bread	uhn urf a la cock *un œuf à la coque* a boiled egg
uhn kaffay krem *un café crème* a white coffee	(shoh/frwa) *(chaud/froid)* (hot/cold)				

Restaurants/Booking a Table

1. *Je voudrais réserver une table pour quatre, pour midi et demie.* I'd like to book a table for four for 12.30.

2. *A quel nom, monsieur?* What name please?

(coping with 'phones p.39)

1. *Avez-vous une table pour trois personnes?*

   Have you a table for three?

2. *Un moment ... Avez-vous réservé?*

   Just a moment ... Have you booked?

Ordering a meal

1. *Je prends / nous prenons le menu à – francs.*

   I/We would like the – franc menu.

2. *Le pâté et le bifteck pour moi – et la soupe et les filets de poisson pour moi.*

   Pâté and steak for me – and soup and fish fillets for me.

3. *Qu'est-ce que vous proposez pour l'enfant / les enfants?*
   (Et un couvert pour le petit)

   What do you suggest for the child/children?
   (And an extra plate for the little one.)

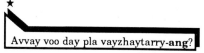

Avez-vous des plats végétariens?
Have you any vegetarian dishes?

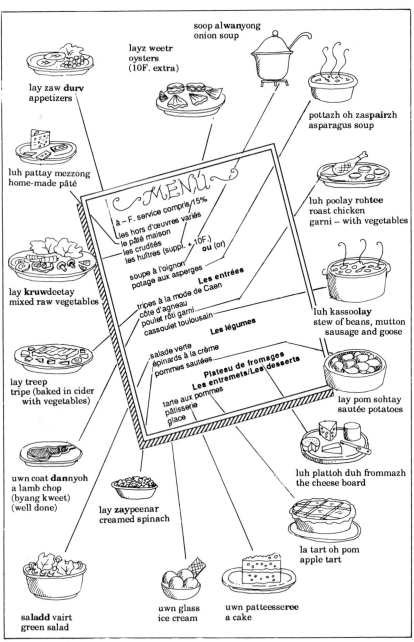

soop al**wan**yong
onion soup

layz weetr
oysters
(10F. extra)

lay zaw **durv**
appetizers

pottazh oh zas**pairzh**
asparagus soup

luh pattay mezzong
home-made pâté

luh poolay roh**tee**
roast chicken
garni – with vegetables

MENU

à – F. service compris 15%
Les hors d'œuvres variés
le pâté maison
les crudités
les huîtres (suppl. + 10F.)   **ou** (or)

soupe à l'oignon
potage aux asperges
                    Les entrées
tripes à la mode de Caen
côte d'agneau
poulet rôti garni
cassoulet toulousain
                    Les légumes
salade verte
épinards à la crème
pommes sautées
          Plateau de fromages
       Les entremets/Les desserts
tarte aux pommes
pâtisserie
glace

lay **kruw**deetay
mixed raw vegetables

luh kassoo**lay**
stew of beans, mutton
sausage and goose

lay treep
tripe (baked in cider
with vegetables)

lay pom soh**tay**
sautée potatoes

uwn coat **dan**nyoh
a lamb chop
(byang k**weet**)
(well done)

lay **zay**peenar
creamed spinach

luh platt**oh** duh frommazh
the cheese board

la tart oh pom
apple tart

sa**ladd** vairt
green salad

uwn glass
ice cream

uwn patteesse**ree**
a cake

Kell ay luh pla duw zhoor?
Quel est le plat du jour?
What is the dish of the day?

You will find a wider choice of meats on p.26, vegetables on p.27 and fish on p.30

Ordering drinks *(boissons)*

1. Musyuh, la kart day vang, seelvooplay.

2. Kuh dayzeeray voo kom bwassong?

4. Gazzurze oo nong gazzurze?

3. Uwn karraff duh vang roozh, dur zhuw duh pom ay uwn bootay doh meenayral, seelvooplay.

1. *Monsieur, la carte des vins, s'il vous plaît.*
   Waiter, may I have the wine list, please.

2. *Que désirez-vous comme boisson?*
   What would you like to drink?

3. *Une carafe de vin rouge, deux jus de pommes et une bouteille d'eau minérale, s'il vous plaît.*
   A carafe of red wine, two apple juices and a bottle of mineral water, please.

4. *Gazeuse ou non gazeuse?*
   Fizzy or still?

Requests and Paying

3. Laddeessyong, seelvooplay. Esskuh luh sairveece ay kompree?

4. Zhuh krwa keel-ya uwn errur don laddeessyong.

1. Musyuh, duh loh, seelvooplay.

2. Ongkor uwn kweeyair, seelvooplay.

uhn kootoh
un couteau
a knife

uwn foorshett
une fourchette
a fork

uwn kweeyair
une cuillère
a spoon

uwn karraff doh
une carafe d'eau
a jug of water

uhn vair
un verre
a glass

1. *Monsieur, de l'eau, s'il vous plaît.*
   Waiter, some water, please.

2. *Encore une cuillère, s'il vous plaît.*
   Another spoon, please.

3. *L'addition, s'il vous plaît. Est-ce que le service est compris?*
   May I have the bill. Is service included?

4. *Je crois qu'il y a une erreur dans l'addition.*
   I think there is a mistake in the bill.

Glass – *Glaces* – Ice cream

oh frezz
aux fraises
strawberry

oh kasseece
au cassis
blackcurrant

oh shokkohla
au chocolat
chocolate

a la peestash
à la pistache
pistachio

a la vanee
à la vanille
vanilla

1. Zhuh voodray uwn glass.

2. Kell parfung voolay voo?

3. Uwn glass oh shokkohla.

4. Uwn sampl oo uwn doobl?

1. *Je voudrais une glace.*
   I'd like an ice cream.

2. *Quel parfum voulez-vous?*
   What flavour would you like?

3. *Une glace au chocolat.*
   A chocolate ice cream.

4. *Une simple ou une double?*
   A single or a double (scoop)?

La cafétéria – le libre-service – le self

Self-service restaurants offer a wide variety of meals. Many have a microwave to heat up your main course after you've eaten your starters. Follow these instructions:

FOUR A MICRO-ONDES
1. Ouvrir la porte en pressant sur le bouton "ouverture de porte".
2. Introduire l'assiette.
3. Fermer la porte.
4. Appuyer sur le bouton "Marche".
5. Attendre le signal sonore.
6. Ouvrir le porte.

MICROWAVE OVEN
1. Press button "**Ouverture de porte**" to open door.
2. Place plate inside.
3. Close door.
4. Press button "**Marche**".
5. Wait for warning buzzer.
6. Open door.

1. Zhuh voodray uhn pur duh suh-la, seelvooplay.

2. Ay day layguwm?

3. Sur-see ay sur-la.

1. *Je voudrais un peu de cela, s'il vous plaît.*
   I'd like some of that, please.

2. *Et des légumes?*
   And what vegetables?

3. *Ceux-ci et ceux-là.*
   These and those.

Special children's menus are often available at good prices though the choice may be rather restricted.   Children's menu — *Menu Enfant.*

SHOPPING

<table>
<tr><td>OUVERT
oovair — open</td><td>FERMÉ
fairmay — closed</td></tr>
</table>

Most shops are open from 9.00 until between 17.30 and 19.00. Many close for lunch, and most food shops close on Mondays.

Groceries: Look for *Alimentation* or *Épicerie* — or the *supermarché* (supermarket). *Libre service* means self-service. You will often find the *hypermarché* (hypermarket) in the *Centre Commercial*. Many places have a *marché* (market) on Sunday mornings.

HOW TO ASK

Voo**zavv**ay (day pom)?	Say kombyang?	**Sussee/sulla**
Vous avez (des pommes)?	*C'est combien?*	*Ceci /cela*
Have you (any apples)?	How much is it/are they?	This/that one

Zhuh voodray — uhn keelo duh (tom**matt**)
Je voudrais — *un kilo de (tomates)*
I'd like — a kilo of (tomatoes)

uwn leevr duh (pesh)
une livre de (pêches)
1lb. of (peaches)

dur song sangkont gram
deux cents cinquante grammes
250g. (about 8oz.)

uwn tronsh duh —	uhn morsoh duh —	ongkor uhn puh-**tee** pur.
Une tranche de —	*Un morceau de —*	*Encore un petit peu.*
A slice of —	A piece of —	A little more.

la **mwa**-teeay/uhn duh-mee	sa suw**fee**?
La moitié/Un demi	*Ça suffit?*
Half	Is that enough?

say troh.	Assay! *Assez!*	
C'est trop.	Sa va. Ça va.	} That's enough.
That's too much.	Sa suw**fee**. *Ça suffit.*	

la pièce	*en reclame*	*du pays*
Each	Special offer	Local produce

IMPORTANT

Use the pattern of conversation shown in the bakery for all other kinds of shopping.

It is good manners in France to say "Bong**zhoor**" *(Bonjour)* on entering a shop, and "Oh **vwahr**" *(Au voir)* when leaving.

Boolongzhe**ree** – *Boulangerie* – Baker

1. *Bonjour, madame.*
   Good day.

3. *Du pain, s'il vous plaît.*
   Je voudrais un pain comme cela.
   Some bread, please.
   I'd like a loaf like that one.

2. *Bonjour, madame, qu'est-ce que vous désirez?*
   Good day. What would you like?

1. *Et trois croissants.*
   And three croissants.

3. *Non, c'est tout. Ça fait combien?*
   No, that's all. How much is that?

2. *Voilà madame. Vous voulez autre chose?*
   There you are. Would you like anything else?

4. *Ça c'est – francs.*
   That's – francs.

24

Patteesse**ree** – *Pâtisserie* – Cakes and sweets
Boulangeries also sell sweets

1. *Je voudrais des bonbons /*
   chocolats aussi.
   I'd like some **sweets/chocolates**
   too.

2. *Oui. C'est pour offrir?*
   Fine. Are they for a present?

   (Say: wee/*oui*/yes, and they
   will be suitably wrapped)

ON LEAVING, SAY: Oh **vwahr**, ma-**dam**.
Au voir, madame.
Goodbye.

WEIGHTS AND MEASURES

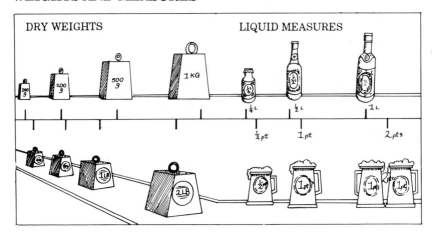

25

Always remember: "Bong**zhoor,** zhuh voodray ..."

Sharkuwte**ree** – *Charcuterie* – Pork butcher/delicatessen

duw por
du porc
some pork

day soh**seece**
des saucisses
some sausages

duw pizza
du pizza
some pizza

duw sohsee**song**
du saucisson
slicing sausage

mair-gay
merguez
spicy lamb
sausage

duw **boo**dang
du boudin
black pudding

duw zhombong
du jambon
some ham

day zaw **durv**
des hors d'œuvres
appetizers

duw pattay
du pâté
some pâté

day **kruw**deetay
des crudités
mixed raw
vegetables

Boosh**eree** – *Boucherie* – Butcher

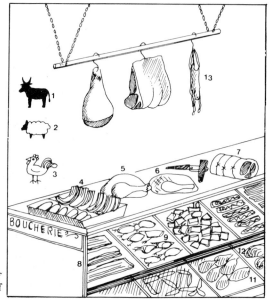

duw burf
du bœuf
some beef

duh lannyoh
de l'agneau
some lamb

day voll-**eye**
des volailles
some poultry

day kottuh**lett**
des côtelettes
some chops

duw poolay
du poulet
some chicken

uhn kannahr
un canard
a duck

duw rohtee
duh burf
du rôti de bœuf
some roast beef

day treep
des tripes
some tripe

duw **zhee**beeyay
du gibier
some game

duw sohtay duh
voh
du sauté de veau
some stewing veal

day zeskal**lop**
des escalopes
some escalopes

duh la vee-**ahnd**
ashay
*de la viande
hachée*
some mince

duw **lap**pang
du lapin
some rabbit

Groceries — *Alimentation* — *Èpicerie*
in *English* order

duh la bee-**air**
de le BIÈRE
some Beer

day biskwee
des BISCUITS
some Biscuits

duw bur
du BEURRE
some Butter

duw shom**pan**ya
du CHAMPAGNE
some Champage

duw frommazh (duh shevr)
du FROMAGE (de chèvre)
some (goat's) Cheese

duw kaffay
du CAFÉ
some Coffee

duh la krem
de la CRÈME
some Cream

day zur
des ŒUFS
some Eggs

duw zhuw duh frwee
du JUS DE FRUITS
some Fruit Juice

duw mee-**ell**
du MIEL
some Honey

duh la kongfee**tuwr**
de la CONFITURE
some Jam

duh la margha**reen**
de la MARGARINE
some Margarine

duw lay
du LAIT (demi)-écrémé)
some Milk (semi)-skimmed)

Zhuh voodray …
Je voudrais …
I'd like …

duh lweel
de L'HUILE
some Oil

duw ree
du RIZ
some Rice

duw suwkr
du SUCRE
some Sugar

duw tay
du THÉ
some Tea

duw papp-yay eezhee-ay**neek**
du PAPIER HYGIÉNIQUE
some Toilet Paper

duh la less**eev**
de la LESSIVE
some Soap Powder

duh loh
de L'EAU
some Water

duw vang roozh/blong
du VIN rouge/blanc
some red/white Wine

day ya-**oor**
des YAOURTS
some Yoghurts

duw sell
du SEL
some Salt

duw pwahvr
du POIVRE
some Pepper

duh la mootard
de la MOUTARDE
some Mustard

Vegetables — *Légumes* (Lay**guwm**)

day **zahr**teeshoh
des ARTICHAUTS
some Artichokes

day zoh-bairzheen
des AUBERGINES
some Aubergines

day **zarr**ikoh vair
des HARICOTS VERTS
some Green Beans

uhn shoo
un CHOU
a Cabbage

day ka**rrott**
des CAROTTES
some Carrots

uhn shoo**flur**
un CHOU-FLEUR
a Cauliflower

duw selree
du CÉLERI
some Celery

duw mah-eess
du MAÏS
some Corn

day koor**zhett**
des COURGETTES
some Courgettes

uhn kawng-kawmbr
un CONCOMBRE
a Cucumber

duh lie
de L'AIL
some Garlic

day pwarroh
des POIREAUX
some Leeks

in *English* order

day pom
des POMMES
some Apples

day **za**breekoh
des ABRICOTS
some Apricots

Fruit & Vegetables

Zhuh voodray …
Je voudrais …
I'd like …

TOMAT.

day **lon**tee
des LENTILLES
some Lentils

uwn lay**tuw**
une LAITUE
a Lettuce

day **sho**mpeenyong
des CHAMPIGNONS
some Mushrooms

day wanyong
des OIGNONS
some Onions

day puh-tee pwa
des PETITS POIS
some Peas

uhn pwahr-vrong
un POIVRON
a Pepper

28

Fruit — *Fruits* (Frwee)

day ban**nan**
des BANANES
some Bananas

uhn pompla-moose
un PAMPLEMOUSSE
a Grapefruit

uhn seetrong
un CITRON
a Lemon

day suh-**reez**
des CERISES
some Cherries

day rezzang
des RAISINS
some Grapes

uhn muh-long
un MELON
a Melon

day bruwn-yong
des BRUGNONS
some Nectarines

day zo**ronzh**
des ORANGES
some Oranges

day pesh
des PÊCHES
some Peaches

day pwahr
des POIRES
some Pears

uhn anna-na
un ANANAS
a Pineapple

day frongbwaz
des FRAMBOISES
some Raspberries

day grohzay
des GROSEILLES
some Redcurrants

day frezz
des FRAISES
some Strawberries

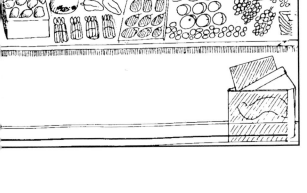

day pom duh tair
des POMMES DE TERRE
some Potatoes

day tom**matt**
des TOMATES
some Tomatoes

day **zay**peenar
des EPINARDS
some Spinach

uhn sack
UN SAC
a Bag

Pwassong
Fish

Frwee duh **Mair**
Seafood

duh la
lee**mahnd**
de la limande
some dab

uwn trweet
une truite
a trout

dayz weetr
des huîtres
some oysters

duw ommar
du hommard
some lobster

duw kalmar
du calmar
some squid

POISSONS-FRUITS DE MER

day zes**kar**goh
des escargots
some snails

duw
kabbeeyoh
du cabillaud
some cod

duw krab
du crabe
some crab

day mool
des moules
some mussels

duw **soh**mong
du saumon
some salmon

Watch out for **Boucherie Chevaline**
and this sign

BOUCHERIE ⌁ CHEVALINE

This is a horse-meat butcher. Whilst horse
may taste fine, we've no idea how long you
need to cook it, and if you really want to try,
you'd better find out how it's done first. All our
books on French cookery maintain a discreet
silence about it!

Confection – Vêtements – **Clothes**

Promotion – Special Offer   *Prix Choc* – Special Offer   *Soldes* – Sale

1. *Bonjour, je voudrais une chemise.*
   Good day, I'd like a blouse/shirt.

2. *Oui. Quelle taille portez-vous?*
   Fine. What size do you take?

3. *Je fais du 40. Pouvez-vous prendre mes mesures?*
   I take size 40. Can you measure me?

1. Pweezh les**say**ay?
   Puis-je l'essayer?
   May I try it on?

2. Byang suwr. Par ee-see, ma-**dam**.
   Bien sûr. Par ici, madame.
   Of course. This way, madam.

3. *Ça ne me va pas.*   4. *C'est trop grand.* 5. *C'est trop petit.*   6. *C'est trop cher.*
   It doesn't fit me.   It's too big.   It's too small.   It's too dear.

Prix choc (Pree shock) has nothing to do with chocolates! It means Special Offer – which doesn't mean you <u>won't</u> get a shock when you see the price, even so!

Methods of payment

1. Sa va tray byang.
   Zhuh luh prahn.
   Sa fay kombyang?

2. Voolay voo payay a la kess.

3. Akseptay voo lay kart duh kray**dee**/ zuroh**shekk**/ shekk duh vwa-**yazh**?

4. Mair**see**.

5. Zhuh voozon **pree**.

1. *Ça va très bien.*
   Je le prends.
   Ça fait combien?
   It fits very well.
   I'll take it.
   How much is it?

3. *Acceptez-vous les cartes de crédit/ eurochèques/chèques de voyage?*
   Do you take credit cards/ Eurocheques/travellers' cheques?

2. *Voulez-vous payer à la caisse.*
   Please pay at the cash desk.

4. *Merci.*
   Thank you.

5. *Je vous en prie.*
   Not at all.

uhn bonnay
un bonnet
a (woolly) hat

uhn shappoh
un chapeau
a hat

uwn shuh-**meeze**
une chemise
a shirt/blouse

uhn ampairmay-**ahbl**
un imperméable
a raincoat

uhn **ponta**-long
un pantalon
some trousers

uhn short
un short
some shorts

day gahn
des gants
some gloves

uwn zhuwp
une jupe
a skirt

uwn rob
une robe
a dress

day **kollon**
des collants
some tights

uhn puwl
un pull
a jumper

uwn sang**tuwr**
une ceinture
a belt

uhn my-oh duh bang
un maillot de bain
a swimming costume

day sond**al**
des sandales
some sandals

day shoh**set**
des chaussettes
some socks

uhn mooshwahr
un mouchoir
a handkerchief

day shoh**suwr**
des chaussures
some shoes

32

CLOTHING SIZES

WOMEN
Dresses/Suits

British	34	36	38	40	42	44	
Continental	40	42	44	46	48	50	

Stockings

British	8	8½	9	9½	10	10½
Continental	0	1	2	3	4	5

Shoes

British	4	5	6	7	8	9
Continental	37	38	39	41	42	43

MEN
Suits/Coats

British	36	38	40	42	44	46
Continental	46	48	50	52	54	56

Shoes

Brit.	5	6	7	8	9	10	11
Cont.	38	39	41	42	43	44	45

Shirts

British	14	14½	15	15½	16	16½
Continental	36	37	38	39	41	42

PHARMACIE – Fahrma-**see** – Chemist

The *Pharmacie* sells mostly drugs and medicines.
Toiletries are sold in the *Droguerie*.

Zhuh voodray kellkuh shoze poor –
Je voudrais quelque chose pour –
I'd like something for –

la kongstee-**pass**yong	uwn too	la dee-ar**ray**
la Constipation	*une Toux*	*la Diarrhée*
Constipation	a Cough	Diarrhoea

luh mal oh zor**ray**
le Mal aux Oreilles
Earache

luh ruwm day fwang
le Rhume des Foins
Hay Fever

luh mal duh tett
le Mal de Tête
Headache

uhn peekuwr dan**sekt**
un Piqûre d'Insecte
an Insect Bite

luh mal duh mair
le Mal de Mer
Seasickness

uhn mal duh gorzh
un Mal de Gorge
a Sore Throat

luh mal **dest**oh-ma
le Mal d'Estomac
Stomach Ache

uhn koo duh sol**lay**
un Coup de Soleil
Sunburn

Emergency chemist: *service de garde / d'urgence* or *pharmacie de service* will tell you which chemist is open out of hours.

(see also Medical Section p.58 and Parts of the Body p.61)

DROGUERIE
Toiletries

Zhuh voodray ...
Je voudrais ...
I'd like ... ★

duw kottong
du COTTON
some Cotton Wool

duh la krem onteesep**teek**
de la CREME ANTISÈPTIQUE
some Antiseptic Cream

duw shompwang
du SHAMPOOING
some Shampoo

day sairvee-**ett**/
tompong eezhee-ay**neek**
*des SERVIETTES/
TAMPONS HYGIÉNIQUES*
Sanitary Towels/Tampons

duh laspee**reen**
de l'ASPIRINE
some Aspirin

day prayzairva-**teef**
des PRÉSERVATIFS
some Condoms

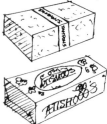

day mooshwahr on papp-yay
des MOUCHOIRS EN PAPIE
Paper Handkerchiefs

uhn razzwahr
un RASOIR
a Razor

uwn bond vel-poh
une BANDE VELPEAU
a Crepe Bandage

day koosh
des COUCHES
some Nappies

day poncemong
des PANSEMENTS
some Sticking Plasters

du la krem ontee-an**sekt**
de la CRÈME ANTI-INSEC
some Insect Repellant

day **zal**-eemong poor baybay
des ALIMENTS POUR BÉBÉ
some Baby Food

duw **savv**
du SAVON
some Soap

duw dontee**freece**
du DENTIFRICE
some Toothpaste

day luw**nett** duh sol**lay**
des LUNETTES DE SOLEIL
some Sunglasses

uwn bross a dong
une BROSSE À DENTS
a Toothbrush

uhn penyuh
un PEIGNE
a Comb

uhn day-**ohdorong**
un DÉODORANT
a Deodorant

duh lweel sol**lair**
de L'HUILE SOLAIR
some Suntan Oil

34

WHO SELLS WHAT

Maison de la Presse — Librairie
Bookshop — Stationery — Newspapers

uhn leevr
un LIVRE
a Book

uwn kart
une CARTE
a Map

ı deeks-yon**air**
DICTIONNAIRE
)ictionary
(fronsay-onglay)
(français-anglais)
(French-English)

uwn pelleekuwl
une PELLICULE
a Film

uhn steeloh
un STYLO
a Pen

uhn zhoornal (onglay)
un JOURNAL (anglais)
an (English) newspaper

uhn krayong
un CRAYON
a Pencil

Tabac — Journaux
Tobacconist — Newspapers

hn tambr
n TIMBRE
Stamp

day kart poss**tal**
des CARTES POSTALES
some Postcards

Quincaillerie
Hardware

uhn oovr bwat
un OUVRE-BOÎTES
a Tin Opener

uwn bootay
(kartoosh) duh gaz
*une BOUTEILLE
(CARTOUCHE) DE GAZ*
Gas Bottle (Cartridge)

day zalluw**mett**
des ALLUMETTES
some Matches

y seega**rett**
CIGARETTES
ne Cigarettes
avvek/song feeltr)
avec / sans filtre)
with/without filter)

uhn breekay
un BRIQUET
a Lighter

uwn lomp duh posh
une LAMPE DE POCHE
a Torch

uwn peel
une PILE
a Battery

duw feel
DU FIL
some Thread

uhn teer booshong
un TIRE-BOUCHON
a Corkscrew

hn toornuh**veece**
n TOURNEVIS
Screwdriver

uwn ay**gwee**
une AIGUILLE
a Needle

day seezoh
des CISEAUX
some Scissors

uhn day-capsuw**lur**
un DÉCAPSULEUR
a Bottle Opener

duh la fee**sell**/kord
de la FICELLE / CORDE
some String/Rope

uwn posh-ett duh glass
une POCHETTE DE GLACE
an Ice Pack

35

BANKS

BANK HOURS are roughly 9.00-12.00 and 14.00-17.30. They close on Saturdays and/or Mondays, also on public holidays and part of the day before.

You can usually change money or traveller's cheques at a bank like these ...

... but not always at one like this – it's a savings bank only.

Public Holidays – Jours Fériés

F	New Years Day	Jan.	1	B/CH
		Jan.	2	CH
F	Easter Monday			B/CH
F	Labour Day	May	1	B
F	VE Day	May	8	
F	Ascension Day			B/CH
F	Whit Monday			B/CH
F	Bastille Day	July	14	
	National Day	July	21	B
	National Day	Aug.	1	CH
F	Assumption	Aug.	15	B
F	All Saints Day	Nov.	1	B
F	Remembrance Day	Nov.	11	B
F	Christmas Day	Dec.	25	B/CH
	St. Stephens Day	Dec.	26	CH

There may be other local holidays.

F — France   B — Belgium   CH — Switzerland

Bank: *Banque, (Bureau de) Change*

1. *Excusez-moi, où est la banque la plus proche?*
   Excuse me, where is the nearest bank?

2. *C'est là-bas, sur la place.*
   It's over there, in the square.

Currency: 1 franc = 100 centimes

la monnay
la monnaie
small change

uhn **bee**yay
un billet
a note

SONNER
ring

POUSSER
push

Je voudrais changer des eurochèques (livres).
Je voudrais toucher un chèque de voyage.
   I'd like to change some Eurocheques (pounds).
   I'd like to cash a traveller's cheque.

Voulez-vous signer ici.
   Please sign here.

2. *Votre passeport, s'il vous plaît.*
   Your passport, please.

4. *Vous pouvez prendre l'argent à la caisse.*
   Please collect the money from the cashier.

Post Office — *P.T.T.*

Où est le bureau de poste, s'il vous plaît?
Where is the post office, please?

Buying Stamps — *Timbres*

Stamps can be bough
at sweet and cigarett
shops (Tabac) – bu
them at the same tim
as your postcards. Som
larger post offices wil
change money and cas
Eurocheques – look fo
"Change" signs. Sinc
both are within th
EEC, the postage rat
for Britain is the sam
as within France.

1. *Je voudrais des timbres pour
   cette lettre / carte postale.*
   I'd like some stamps for this
   letter/postcard.

2. *Ça coûte combien?*
   How much is it?

Telephone — *Téléphone* (taylay**fonn**)

Oo ay luh taylay**fonn** (luh pluw prosh)? ★

★ Pweezh uwtee**lee**zay votr taylay**fonn**?

*Où est le téléphone
(le plus proche)?*
Where is the (nearest)
phone?

*Puis-je utiliser votre
téléphone?*
May I use your phone,
please?

Instructions:

Décrochez le combiné —lift the receiver
Composez le numéro —dial the number
(Numerotez —dial the number)
(Patientez svp —please wait)
Introduisez les pièces —insert coins
(Retirez votre carte —take card)
(or press *retrait carte*)

Cardphone *(Publiphone à carte)*
Many phones are card-operated.
TÉLÉCARTES are obtainable from
post offices, newsagents, etc.

Not all phone boxes can make
international calls. The post office,
counter marked **téléphone** will
allocate you a **cabine.** Pay when you
finish.

RINGING HOME: To ring Britain,
dial 19, wait for a second tone, dial 44
and then the local code (leave off the
first 0).

For

U.S. & Canada .... dial 19 then	1
Australia .... dial 19 then	61
New Zealand .... dial 19 then	64
Eire .... dial 19 then	353

(For an English-speaking operator dial
(G.B.) 19 00 44 or (U.S.A.) 19 00 11).

3. Zhuh voodray parlay a —
4. Nuh keetay pa!
1. Zhuh voodray taylayfonnay on Ongluh**tair.**
2. Zhuh voodray fair uhn ap**pel** on Pay Say Vay.

1. *Je voudrais téléphoner en Angleterre.*
   I'd like to ring England.

2. *Je voudrais faire un appel en PCV.*
   I'd like to make a reverse-charge
   (collect) call.

3. *Je voudrais parler à —*
   May I speak to — please?

4. *Ne quittez pas!*
   Please hold on.

Telegrams — *Télégrammes*

2. **Rom**pleessay set feesh, seelvoo**play.**
1. Zhuh voodray ong**vwa**-yay uhn taylay**gram** a Grond Bruh**tan**yuh.
3. Kell ay luh pree par moh?

1. *Je voudrais envoyer un télégramme
   en Grande Bretagne.*
   I'd like to send a telegram to
   Great Britain.

2. *Remplissez cette fiche, s'il vous
   plaît.*
   Fill in this form, please.

3. *Quel est le prix par mot?*
   How much is it per word?

Finding the way

luh shatto
le château
the chateau

(komping) antair**dee**
(camping) interdit
(camping) forbidden

la zho
la

nor
NORD
north

GENDARMERIE

CAFE

BANQUE

GARE SNCF

CAMPING INTERDIT

est
EST
east

le musée

suwd
SUD
south

Oo ay?
Ou est?
Where is?
(If more than one,
say: Oo song?
Where are?)

la gahr
la gare
the station

lay**gleez**
l'église
the church

luh muwzay
le musée
the museum

la plass
la place
the square

40

luh marshay
le marché
the market

lay **mag**gazang
les magasins
the shops

loh**tell**
l'hôtel
the hotel

la reev-**yair**
la rivière
the river

station

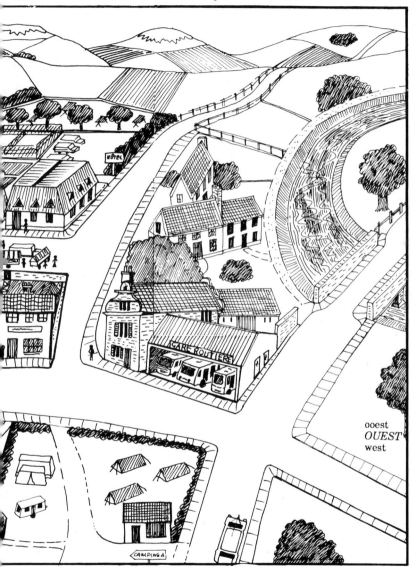

ooest
OUEST
west

eeka
icat d'Initiative

uh Too**reezm**
e de Tourisme
ourist Office

mair-ee (or) oh**tell** duh vee
Marie (or) *Hôtel de Ville*
Town Hall

la gahr rooty-**air**
la gare routière
the bus station

luh pong
le pont
the bridge

★
> Poor allay a —, seelvoo**play**?
> *Pour aller à —, s'il vous plaît?*
> How do I get to —, please?

41

1. *Excusez-moi, où est la rue de –?*
   Excuse me, where is – street?

2. *Traversez la rue et prenez la première à droite.*
   Cross the road and take the first right.

3. *Pouvez-vous me montrer sur la carte où je suis?*
   Could you show me on the map where I am?

Directions

too drwa
tout droit
straight on

a drwatt
à droite
to the right

a goshe
à gauche
to the left

Gents
Hommes
Messieurs

Ladies
Dames
Femmes

lay twa-**lett**
les toilettes
the toilets **WC**

Libre
Occupé
Hors service
Vacant
Engaged
Out of order

Locations

lay fur
les feux
traffic lights

a kohtay duh
à côté de
next to

on fass duh
en face de
opposite

oh kwang
au coin
on the corner

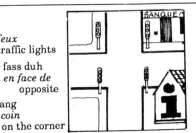

derry-**air**
derrière
behind

pray (duh)
près (de)
near (to)

luh karfoor
le carrefour
the crossroads

Road Travel

What kind of road traveller are you?

la moto / le scooter
the motorbike/the scooter

lohtoh/la vwa**tuwr**
l'auto / la voiture
the car

luh buwss (luh kar)
le bus (le car)
the bus (the coach)

luh **vay**lo
le vélo
the bicycle

uhn taxi
un taxi
a taxi

(une station de taxis)
(a taxi rank)

zhuh marsh
je marche
I walk

Priorité à droite

Traffic from the right generally has right of way.

Before you start off driving, remember that *unless you see a sign that says otherwise,* ALL traffic coming from your right has priority. Don't be surprised if a tractor driver pulls out from a farm track on your right without looking – he's allowed to, and you are expected to give way. Don't get flustered – be prepared. Here are a few signs that show who has right of way. Note that buses usually have right of way when leaving their stops.

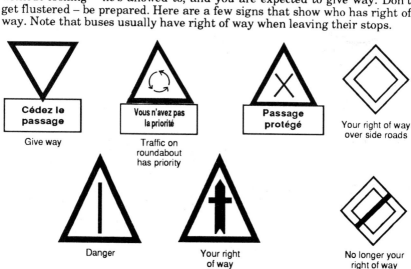

Cédez le passage — Give way

Vous n'avez pas la priorité — Traffic on roundabout has priority

Passage protégé

Your right of way over side roads

Danger

Your right of way

No longer your right of way

In Town

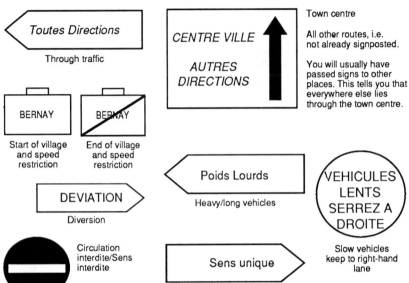

Toutes Directions

Through traffic

CENTRE VILLE

AUTRES DIRECTIONS

Town centre

All other routes, i.e. not already signposted.

You will usually have passed signs to other places. This tells you that everywhere else lies through the town centre.

BERNAY

Start of village and speed restriction

BERNAY

End of village and speed restriction

DEVIATION

Diversion

Poids Lourds

Heavy/long vehicles

VEHICULES LENTS SERREZ A DROITE

Slow vehicles keep to right-hand lane

Circulation interdite/Sens interdite

No entry

Sens unique

One-way street

Parking Signs

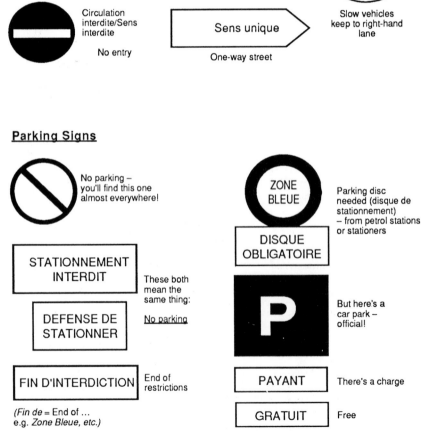

No parking – you'll find this one almost everywhere!

STATIONNEMENT INTERDIT

DEFENSE DE STATIONNER

These both mean the same thing:

No parking

FIN D'INTERDICTION

End of restrictions

(Fin de = End of ...
e.g. Zone Bleue, etc.)

ZONE BLEUE

DISQUE OBLIGATOIRE

Parking disc needed (disque de stationnement) – from petrol stations or stationers

P

But here's a car park – official!

PAYANT

There's a charge

GRATUIT

Free

Motorways – Autoroutes

Péage means toll

Need change?
— take lane
marked *monnaie*

A10
Péage

SORTIE exit

Aire de – lay-by or service area

Don't forget –
seatbelts
*(ceintures de
securité)* are
compulsory

On the open road

GRAVILLONS

loose chippings

**CHAUSSEE
DEFORMEE**

poor road surface

DOUANE

DOUANE – Customs

You've reached the end
of the (French) road!

**BREST
Itinéraire bis**

**BREST
Itinéraire bis**

Alternative (holiday) route
avoiding major traffic jams

**RISQUE DE
VERGLAS**

Danger of skidding

Fire danger – do not
light fires, matches,
cigarettes, etc.,
where you see this
sign

Dégustation 150m
→

Dégustation means "Tasting". Somewhere
nearby someone is selling wine, usually
local produce. Occasionally it's local foods
too, with samples to encourage you to buy.

ATTENTION!

Danger – watch out!

Bong vwa-**yazh!**
Bon voyage!
Have a good journey!

Petrol Station/Garage

Où est la station service la plus proche?
Where is the nearest petrol station?

Fuel: les**once**
   l'essence
    petrol (also
    2-star grade)

luh suwpair
 le super
  4-star grade
  petrol

luh deezel/gazzoil
 le diesel / gasoil
  diesel

luh may**lonzh duh** tom
 le mélange deux
 temps
  2-stroke mixture

lweel loh
l'huile *l'eau*
 oil water

les**once** song plom
l'essence sans plomb
lead-free petrol

1. *Combien d'essence voulez-vous?*
 How much petrol would you
 like?

3. *Pouvez-vous vérifier l'huile?*
 Please check the oil.

2. *Le plein du super / de la normale /*
 sans plomb / du gasoil (OR –
 litres).
  Fill it up with super/normal/
  lead-free/diesel (OR – litres).

4. *Ça coûte combien?*
 How much is that?

libre service — self-service

Faire la vidange
To change the oil

46

Breakdowns/Repairs

Help — *Secours*

Look for orange emergency phone marked *Secours Routier* or phone sign and *Gendarmerie*.

(Fire Brigade — *Pompiers*)

Je suis en panne.
Puis-je me servir de votre téléphone?

> I have broken down.
> May I use your phone?

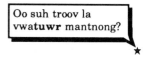

Où se trouve la voiture maintenant?

> Where is the car now?

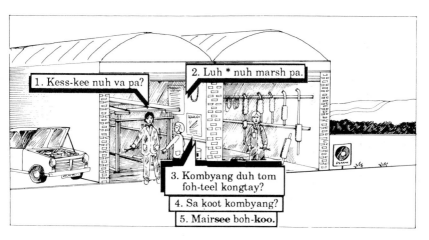

1. *Qu'est-ce qui ne va pas?*
   What's the matter?

2. *Le *– ne marche pas.*
   The *– isn't working.

3. *Combien de temps faut-il compter?*
   How long will it take?

4. *Ça coûte combien?*
   How much is it?

5. *Merci beaucoup.*
   Thank you very much.

*For a selection of car components and things that might go wrong, see page 48.

On Two and Four Wheels

Zhay buzzwang duhn —
J'ai besoin d'un —
I need a —

Luh mot**tur** shoaf (a day rattay).
Le moteur chauffe (a des ratés).
The engine is overheating (misfiring).

La vwat**uwr** kal.
La voiture cale.
The engine is stalling.

Luh — nuh marsh pa.
Le — ne marche pas.
The — isn't working.

Car, Bicycle and Motorcycle parts (in *English* order)

1. luh feeltr a air
   le filtre à air
      the Air Filter

2. la bat**tree**
   la batterie
      the Battery

3. lay frang
   les freins
      the Brakes

4. lay pattang duh frang
   les patins de frein
      the Brake Blocks

5. uwn om**pool**
   une ampoule
      a Bulb

6. luh kahbl duh frang
   (vee**tess**)
      le câble de frein
      (vitesse)
         the Brake (Gear)
         Cable

7. luh karbuwrat**tur**
   le carburateur
      the Carburettor

8. la shen
   la chaîne
      the Chain

9. luh start**air**
   le starter
      the Choke

10. lonbr-eye-**azh**
    l'embrayage
       the Clutch

11. la-luw**mur**
    l'allumeur
       the Distributor

12. luh see**stem**
    aylek**treek**
       le système électrique
       the Electrical
       System

13. luh mot**tur**
    le moteur
       the Engine

14. lay**shapp**mong
    l'échappement
       the Exhaust

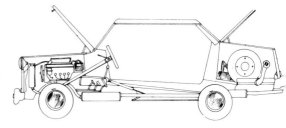

15. la koor**wa** duh
    vonteelat**tur**
       la courroie de
       ventilateur
          the Fan Belt

16. luh kahdr
    le cadre
       the Frame

17. la foorsh avvong
    la fourche avant
       the Front Fork

18. uhn fuwzeebl
    un fusible
       a Fuse

19. uhn zhwang
    un joint
       the Gasket

20. luh shonzhmong duh
    vee**tess**
       le changement de
       vitesse
          the Gear Change

21. luh **gee**dong
    le guidon
       the Handlebars

22. luh fahr
    le phare
       the Headlight

23. uwn shahmbr a air
    une chambre à air
       an Inner Tube

24. la klay
    la clef
       the Key

25. uwn fweet dweel (doh)
    une fuite d'huile
    (d'eau)
       an Oil/Water
       Leak

26. uwn lomp
    une lampe
       a Light

27. luh port bag**gazh**
    le porte-bagages
       Luggage Carrier

28. uhn songdoh
    un sandow
       Luggage Elastic

29. uhn pahr boo
    un pare-boue
       a Mudguard

30. uhn aykroo
    un écrou
       a Nut

31. uhn zherree**kan**
    un jerrican
    a Petrol Can

32. lay vee platteenay
    les vis platinées
    the Points

33. uwn pomp
    une pompe
    a Pump

34. uwn rayparr**rass**yong
    vaylo
    une réparation vélo
    a Puncture Kit

35. luh raddyat**tur**
    le radiateur
    the Radiator

36. uwn sak**kosh**
    une sacoche
    Saddlebag/
    Pannier

37. uwn veece
    une vis
    a Screw

38. uhn toornuh**veece**
    un tournevis
    a Screwdriver

39. uhn ammortees**sur**
    un amortisseur
    a Shock Absorber

40. luh poh
    day**shap**pmong
    le pot
    d'échappement
    the Silencer

41. uwn klay (a aykroo)
    une clef (à écrous)
    a Spanner

42. uwn boo**zhee**
    une bougie
    a Sparking Plug

43. uhn rayong
    un rayon
    a Spoke

44. luh daymar**rur**
    le démarreur
    the Starter

45. uhn p**nur**
    un pneu
    a Tyre

46. la pressyong day
    p**nur**
    la pression des
    pneus
    the Tyre Pressure

47. uwn valve
    une valve
    a Valve

48. uwn r**oo**
    une roue
    a Wheel

49. la zhont
    la jante
    Wheel Rim

50. luh pahr breeze
    le pare-brise
    the Windscreen

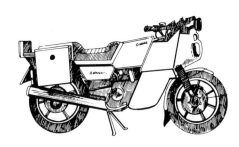

day shen duh nezh
des chaînes de neige
some Snow Chains

uwn kruh-**vezz**ong
une crevaison
a Puncture

uhn kask
un casque
a Crash Helmet

Location de Vélos
Location 2 Roues

Bicycles for Hire

At many French railway
stations you can hire
bikes where you see this
sign: *Train + Vélo*

49

CAR HIRE
Location de voitures

1. *Bonjour madame. Je voudrais louer une voiture.*
   Good day. I would like to hire a car.

2. *Quelle sorte de voiture – petite, moyenne, grande?*
   What sort of car – small, medium, large?

1. *Pour une journée? Pour une semaine?*
   For one day? For one week?

3. *Voici mon permis de conduire.*
   Here is my driving licence.

2. *Quel est le tarif?*
   What is the rate?

4. *Est-ce que je peux rendre la voiture à Lyon?*
   May I leave the car in Lyons?

Buying Tickets: Basic pattern

1. Zhuh voodray uhn **bee**yay oh pru**myair**/duh-**zyem** poor Pa-**ree.**
2. Wee. **Al**-lay, oo **al**-lay ay ruh-**toor**?
3. **Al**-lay sampl. Say kombyang?
4. Zhuh voodray ray**zair**vay uwn plass/koo**shett.**

Voo**zal**-lay **oo**?
Vous allez où?
    Where are you going?

Zhuh vay a –
Je vais à –
    I'm going to –

Station staff wearing an orange band on their cap and sleeve (or an orange scarf in the case of lady staff) will give you any information you need.

1. *Je voudrais un billet en première / deuxième pour Paris.*
   I'd like a first class/second class ticket for Paris.
2. *Oui. Aller, ou aller et retour?*
   OK. Single or return?
3. *Aller simple. C'est combien?*
   Single. How much is it?
4. *Je voudrais réserver une place / couchette.*
   I'd like to reserve a seat/ couchette.

1. *Quel est le quai pour Boulogne?*
   Which is the platform for Boulogne?
2. *Quai numéro trois.*
   Platform three.
3. *A quelle heure part le train?*
   What time does the train go?
4. *A dix heures vingt.*
   At 10.20.

1. Kell ay luh kay poor **Boolon**yuh?

ACCES AUX QUAIS

2. Kay **nuw**mayroh trwa.

4. A **deezur** vang.

3. A kell ur pahr luh trang?

Finding a seat and Local Travel p.54

Rail Travel

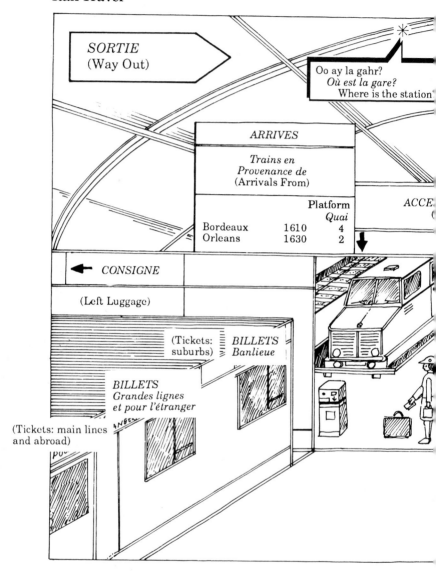

SORTIE
(Way Out)

Oo ay la gahr?
Où est la gare?
Where is the station

ARRIVES		
Trains en Provenance de (Arrivals From)		
		Platform *Quai*
Bordeaux	1610	4
Orleans	1630	2

ACCE

CONSIGNE

(Left Luggage)

(Tickets: suburbs) *BILLETS Banlieue*

BILLETS Grandes lignes et pour l'étranger

(Tickets: main lines and abroad)

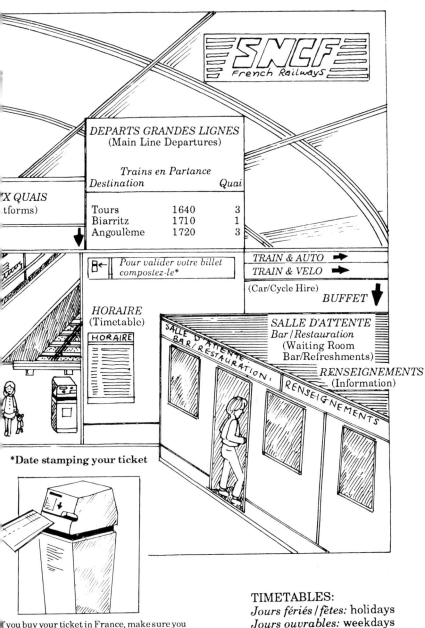

DEPARTS GRANDES LIGNES
(Main Line Departures)

Trains en Partance

Destination		Quai
Tours	1640	3
Biarritz	1710	1
Angoulème	1720	3

X QUAIS
tforms)

B← *Pour valider votre billet*
compostez-le*

HORAIRE
(Timetable)

HORAIRE

*Date stamping your ticket

TRAIN & AUTO ➡
TRAIN & VELO ➡
(Car/Cycle Hire)
BUFFET ⬇

SALLE D'ATTENTE
Bar / Restauration
(Waiting Room
Bar/Refreshments)

RENSEIGNEMENTS
(Information)

SALLE D'ATTENTE
BAR/RESTAURATION, RENSEIGNEMENTS

f you buy your ticket in France, make sure you
tamp (*composter*) it before each leg of your
urney in the orange date-stamping machine
t the platform entrance.

TIMETABLES:
Jours fériés / fêtes: holidays
Jours ouvrables: weekdays
Tous les jours: every day
sauf: except

53

Finding a seat

NON FUMEURS =
No smoking

*This phrase will do just as well for asking about a seat on a bus, plane or park bench – or in a restaurant, theatre, etc.

1. *Cette place, est-elle occupée?* *
   Is this seat taken?

2. *C'est bien le train pour Le Havre?*
   Is this the train for Le Havre?

Local Transport (*Correspondance* — change here for —)

Métro
luh maytroh
  le métro
    the underground/
    subway

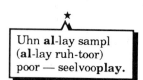

Un aller simple
(aller-retour)
pour — s'il vous plaît.
  A single (return)
  to — please.

1. *Quelle ligne va à Notre Dame?*
   Which line goes to Notre Dame?

2. *Faut-il changer de train?*
   Do I have to change?

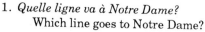

Bus Travel

Remember:

Bus or *autobus*	=	ordinary stopping bus
Car or *autocar*	=	long-distance or tourist coach
Arrêt	=	stop
Vente de Tickets	=	Tickets on sale

Bus tickets can usually be bought on the bus, or from machines at bus stops, or from *tabacs* in large towns. Often you can get a *carnet* (carnay) of 10 or more tickets at a discount.

1. Kon pahr luh buwss poor Vairs-eye?

2. Oo ay larray duh buwss poor la Toor Eefell?

1. *Quand part le bus pour Versailles?*
   When does the bus for Versailles go?

2. *Où est l'arrêt de bus pour la Tour Eiffel?*
   Where is the bus stop for the Eiffel Tower?

la gare = railway station
la gare routière = bus station

Entrée = In
Sortie = Out
(Appuyez =Push i.e. button)

Dwazh dessondr ee-see poor la gahr?

Dois-je descendre ici pour la gare?
Should I get off here for the station?

Air Travel

A la-**air**ohpor
A l'aéroport
　At the airport

lav-yong
l'avion
　the aeroplane

1. Ess keel-**ya** uhn vol poor Zhuh**nairv**?
2. Wee. A nurv-ur deece.
3. A kell ur ay lonruh-**zhee**struh-mong?
4. Kell ay luh **nuw**wayroh duw vol?

1. *Est-ce qu'il y a un vol pour Genève?*
　Is there a flight for Geneva?
2. *Oui. A neuf heures dix.*
　Yes. At 9.10.
3. *A quelle heure est l'enregistrement?*
　What time should I check in?
4. *Quel est le numéro du vol?*
　What is the flight number?

1. Zhuh voodray shonzhay (kong**feer**may/**ann**uwlay) ma rayzair**vass**yong suwr luh vol **nuw**mayroh –.
2. Wee ma-**dam.** Poor kell vol?

1. *Je voudrais changer (confirmer/annuler) ma réservation sur le vol numéro –*
　I'd like to change (confirm/cancel) my reservation on flight number –
2. *Oui madame. Pour quel vol?*
　Yes madam. For which flight?

Boat Travel

A la gahr marry**teem**
A la gare maritime
At the boat terminal

AUX BATEAUX
To the boats

1. **Doo** pahr luh proshang batto poor Bell Eel?

2. Kombyang duh tom duwr la travvairsay?

1. *D'où part le prochain bateau pour Belle-Isle?*
   Where does the next boat for Belle-Isle go from?

2. *Combien de temps dure la traversée?*
   How long does the crossing take?

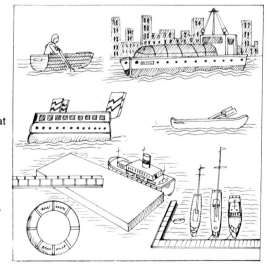

la mair
la mer
the sea

luh lack
le lac
the lake

uwn bark
une barque
a rowing boat

la-airoglees**sur**
l'aéroglisseur
the hovercraft

lombarkad**dair**
l'embarcadère
the landing-stage

luh batto
le bateau
the boat

la sang**tuwr**
la ceinture
the lifebelt

la vuh-**dett**
la vedette
the launch

uhn **kan**nooay
un canoë
a canoe

luh por (duh plez**zonce**)
le port (de plaisance)
the (yacht) harbour

luh canal
le canal
the canal

Accidents and Illness

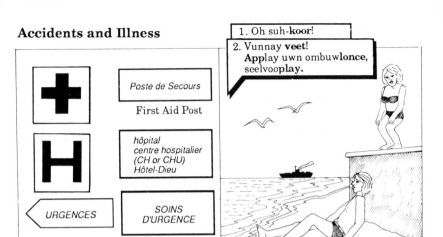

✚	Poste de Secours First Aid Post
H	hôpital centre hospitalier (CH or CHU) Hôtel-Dieu
← URGENCES	SOINS D'URGENCE
Emergencies/ Casualty Department	

1. Oh suh-**koor**!

2. Vunnay **veet**!
   Applay uwn ombuw**lonce**,
   seelvoo**play**.

1. *Au secours!*
   Help!

2. *Venez vite! Appelez une*
   ambulance, s'il vous plaît.
   Come quickly! Please call an
   ambulance.

Minor ailments: See **Pharmacie** section p.33

Calling the doctor/making an appointment

a. Zhuh swee mall**ad**.
   Zhay buzzwang
   duhn maydsang.

b. Zhuh voodray vwahr
   luh maydsang. A kell ur
   pweezh veneer?

Docteur G. GENOUX
Médecine Générale
Consultations
Tous les jours
de 10ᴴ à 12ᴴ

Surgery hours 10-12 daily

Médecin
10, rue Dupont

(Both these signs are for
doctors)

a. *Je suis malade.*
   J'ai besoin d'un médicin.
   I'm ill. I need a doctor

b. *Je voudrais voir le médecin.*
   A quelle heure puis-je venir?
   I'd like to see the doctor.
   When can I come?

If you go to a doctor you will have to pay him on the spot, but if you have brought
Form E111 (from the DSS) with you most of the cost will be refunded by the French
authorities later. However, E111 does not include ambulance charges so it is worth
having an insurance policy to cover these.

At the Doctor's (Parts of the body p.61)

1. *Où avez-vous mal? Cela vous fait mal?*
   Where does it hurt? Does that hurt?

2. *J'ai mal ici. J'ai chaud (froid). J'ai vomi.*
   It hurts here. I am hot (cold). I have been sick.

3. *Êtes-vous vacciné contre le tétanos?*
   Have you been vaccinated against tetanus?

4. *Depuis combien de temps êtes–vous malade?*
   How long have you been ill?

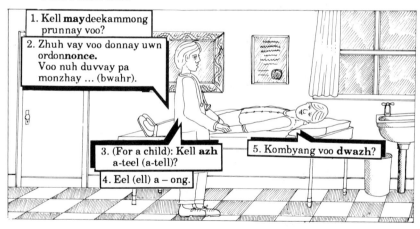

1. *Quel médicament prenez-vous?*
   What medicines do you take?

3. (**For a child**): *Quel âge a-t-il (elle)?*
   How old is he (she)?

4. *Il (elle) a – ans.*
   He (she) is – years old.

2. *Je vais vous donner une ordonnance. Vous ne devez pas manger … (boire).*
   I will give you a prescription. You must not eat … (drink).

5. *Combien vous dois-je?*
   How much do I owe you?

When to take your medicine:	What the doctor needs to know:

When to take your medicine:

... fois par jour
(... times a day)

toutes les ... heures
(every ... hours)

avant/après les repas
(before/after meals)

pendant ... jours
(for ... days)

en cas de douleurs
(if in pain)

98·6° F = 37° C

What the doctor needs to know:

Zhuh swee ... *(Je suis ...)* I'm ...

zallair-**zheek** a
allergique à
allergic to

zasma**teek**
asthmatique
asthmatic

dee-abay**teek**   zaypeelep-**teek**
diabétique   *épileptique*
diabetic   epileptic

zon-**sant**
enceinte
pregnant

zhuh fay dulla tonsyong
Je fais de la tension
I've high blood pressure

zhay dayzon-**wee** kardy-**akk**
J'ai des ennuis cardiaques
I have heart trouble

At the Dentist

Chirurgien-Dentiste
Urgences et Rendez-vous

Emergencies and by appointment

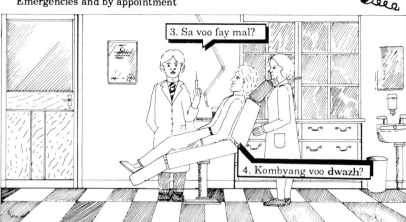

1. Zhay mal oh dong.

2. Pweezh prahndr uhn rondy**voo**?

3. Sa voo fay mal?

4. Kombyang voo **dwazh**?

1. *J'ai mal au dents.*
   I have toothache.

2. *Puis-je prendre un rendez-vous?*
   May I make an appointment?

3. *Ça vous fait mal?*
   Does that hurt?

4. *Combien vous dois-je?*
   How much do I owe you?

Parts of the Body — from top to bottom

la tett
la tête
the head

luh veezazh
le visage
the face

lay shuh-**vur**
les cheveux
the hair

layz yur
les yeux
the eyes

(uhn uh-ee)
(un oeil)
(an eye)

lay zo**rray**
les oreilles
the ears

luh nay
le nez
the nose

la boosh
la bouche
the mouth

lay dong
les dents
the teeth

la gorzh
la gorge
the throat

luh koo
le cou
the neck

lay**pole**
l'épaule
the shoulder

la pwat**treen**
la poitrine
the chest

luh kur
le cœur
the heart

luh doh
le dos
the back

luh bra
le bras
the arm

Luh kor
Le corps
The body

Zhay mal a –
J'ai mal à –
My – hurts

la mang
la main
the hand

luh kood
le coude
the elbow

luh dwa
le doigt
the finger

lestohma
l'estomac
the stomach

la onsh
la hanche
the hip

la zhahmb
la jambe
the leg

luh zhuh-**noo**
le genou
the knee

la shuh-**vee**
la cheville
the ankle

luh pee-**ay**
le pied
the foot

lor**tuh**-ee
l'orteil
the toe

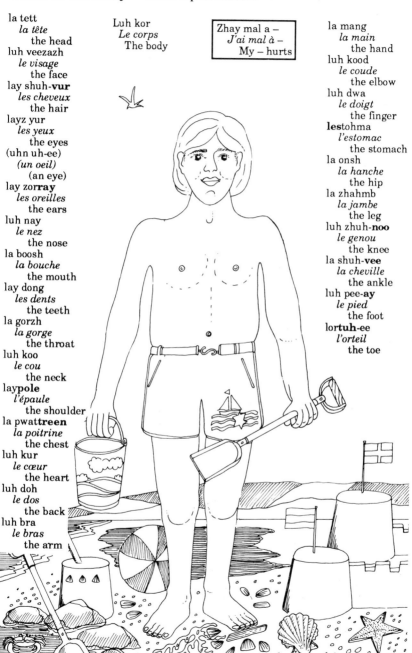

Sightseeing

1. Kess keel-**ya** dantay**res**son ee-**see**?

2. Ong puh **vee**zeetay lay grott, luh shatto …

3. Luh shatto, kon **ay**-suh oo**vair**?

4. Set oo**vair** too lay zhoor sohf lurndee.

Oo ay luh **san**deeka deeneesya-**tee**v?

★

Où est le Syndicat d'Initiative?
   Where is the Tourist Office?

1. *Qu'est-ce qu'il y a d'intéressant ici?*
   Is there anything interesting to see here?

3. *Le château, quand est-ce ouvert?*
   When is the chateau open?

2. *On peut visiter les grottes, le château …*
   You can visit the caves, the chateau …

4. *C'est ouvert tous les jours sauf lundi.*
   It is open every day except Monday.

★

Puh tong ee ontray?

Peut-on y entrer?
May we go in?

1. Avvay voo uhn plon duh veel?

2. Ee a-**teel** uhn geéd kee parl onglay?

| **EXPOSITION** |
| Exhibition |
| **ENTREE LIBRE** |
| Admission Free |

1. *Avez-vous un plan de ville?*
   Have you a town plan?

2. *Y a-t-il un guide qui parle anglais?*
   Is there an English-speaking guide?

Sports

1. Oo puh tong zhooay oh tunny? (footba–l) Kell ay luh tar**reef**?

2. Oo suh troov uhn terrang duh golf? (la plazh/la pee**seen**)

3. Oo suh troov uhn bong ondrwa poor peshay?

4. Esskuh zhay buzzwang duhn pair**mee**?

No swimming

1. *Où peut-on jouer au tennis? (football)*
   Quel est le tarif?

   Where can you play tennis?
   (football). What does it cost?

2. *Où se trouve un terrain de golf?*
   (la plage / la piscine)

   Where is there a golf course?
   (the beach/the swimming pool)

3. *Où se trouve un bon endroit pour*
   pêcher?

   Where is a good place to fish?

4. *Est-ce que j'ai besoin d'un permis?*

   Do l need a permit?

Skiing

luh skee duh fong
le ski de fond
cross-country skiing

Ay**kol** duh skee
Ski school

Location de skis
Ski hire

1. Pweezh prahndr day lussong duh skee?

2. Wee, byang suwr.

3. Zhuh voodray looay duh lay**keep**mong duh skee.

4. Eel muh foh uwn kart dab**bon**nuh-mong oh**see**.

day shoh**suwr** duh skee
des chaussures de ski
some ski boots

day battong
des bâtons
some ski sticks

day skee
des skis
some skis

1. *Puis-je prendre des leçons de ski?*
   Can I take some skiing
   lessons?

2. *Oui, bien sûr.*
   Yes, of course.

3. *Je voudrais louer de l'équipement*
   de ski.
   I'd like to hire some skiing
   equipment.

4. *Il me faut une carte*
   d'abonnement aussi.
   I'll need a lift pass too.

More skiing on next page

Entertainment: Booking tickets

1. A kell ur kommonss luh spek**takk**la?
2. Zhuh voodray uhn/dur beeyay poor samdee swahr.
3. A kell pree?
4. Tront frong, on**veer**ong.

1. Kess kong pass oh **seen**ayma (taya**hr**tra) suh swahr?
★
2. Zhuh voodray vwahr uhn match duh footba-l.
3. Ess keel-**ya** uwn deeskotekk par ee-**see**? ★

1. *À quelle heure commence le spectacle?*
   What time does the performance start?
3. *À quel prix?*
   At what price?

2. *Je voudrais un / deux billets pour samedi soir.*
   I'd like one/two tickets for Saturday evening.
4. *Trente francs, environ.*
   About 30 francs.

1. *Qu'est-ce qu'on passe au cinéma (théâtre) ce soir?*
   What's on at the cinema (theatre) this evening?
2. *Je voudrais voir un match de football.*
   I'd like to see a football match.
3. *Est-ce qu'il y a une discothèque par ici?*
   Is there a disco here?

On the piste

luh **tay**layskee
le téléski
the ski lift

1. Zhuh voodray fair duw skee.

luh taylayfay**reek**
le téléphérique
the cable car

2. Oo song lay peest poor **day**buwtong?

1. *Je voudrais faire du ski.*
   I'd like to go skiing.

2. *Où sont les pistes pour débutants?*
   Where are the beginners' runs?

Making Friends

1. *Bonjour. Quelle belle journée!*
   Comment allez-vous?
   Hello. What a lovely day!
   How are you?
3. *Je m'appelle –.*
   Comment vous appelez-vous?
   My name is –.
   What is your name?

2. *Très bien – et vous?*
   Fine thanks – and you?
4. *Voici mon mari (ma femme),*
   ma fille et mon fils.
   This is my husband (my wife),
   my daughter and my son.
5. *Enchanté.*
   Pleased to meet you.

1. *Voici ma sœur (mon frère).*
   As-tu des frères et des sœurs?
   Here is my sister (my brother).
   Have you any brothers and
   sisters?

2. *Quel âge as-tu?*
   How old are you?
3. *J'ai treize ans.*
   I am 13.

1. *Vos enfants sont très sympathiques. D'où êtes-vous?*
   Your children are very nice. Where do you come from?

3. *Est-ce la première fois que vous venez en France?*
   Is this your first visit to France?

2. *J'habite Londres.*
   I live in London.

4. *Est-ce que vous vous plaisez ici?*
   Do you like it here?

5. *Oui, beaucoup.*
   Yes, very much.

Accepting an Invitation

Only London (Lawndr/*Londres*), Edinburgh (**Ay**damboor/*Edimbourg*) and Dover (Doovr/*Douvres*) are translated into French. All other places in the British Isles and the rest of the English-speaking world have their names unchanged by the French (more or less ...).

1. *Pouvez-vous venir chez nous ce soir?*
   Would you like to come and see us this evening?

2. *Vous êtes très gentil. Je viendrai avec plaisir.*
   That's very nice of you. I'd be glad to.

Visiting

1. *Asseyez-vous, je vous en prie.*
   Servez-vous.
   Please sit down. Help yourself.

2. *Aimez-vous les sports / la lecture /*
   danser / la musique / jouer aux cartes?
   Do you like sport/reading/
   dancing/music/playing cards?

3. *J'aime bien ...*
   I like ...

4. *C'était très bon, merci.*
   That was very nice, thank
   you.

Saying Goodbye

1. *Merci pour la soirée.*
   C'était formidable.
   Thank you for this evening.
   It was wonderful.

2. *Au revoir.*
   Goodbye.

Pests

If you don't fancy the local Casanova, one of these *might* work. If it doesn't, you could try half a brick hidden in your handbag ...

1. **Less**ay-mwa tron**kee**!
2. **Al**-lay voo**zong**!

1. *Laissez-moi tranquille!*
   Leave me alone!

2. *Allez-vous-en!*
   Go away!

Theft and lost property

1. *J'ai perdu (mon passeport).*
   I've lost (my passport).

2. *On m'a volé (mon passeport).*
   (My passport) has been stolen.

3. *Comment est-ce? Qu'est-ce qu'il y avait dedans?*
   What does it look like? What was in it?

1. Zhay pairduw (mong passpor).
2. Ong ma vollay (mong passpor).

3. Kommon **ay**-suh? Kess keel yavvay duh-dong?

mong sack	mong arzhong	may clay
mon sac	*mon argent*	*mes clefs*
my Bag	my Money	my Keys
mong portfuh-ee	may shekk duh vwa-**yazh**	mong appa-ray photo
mon portefeuille	*mes chèques de voyage*	*mon appareil-photo*
my Wallet	my Travellers' Cheques	my Camera

nom	a-**dress**	kon	oo	
nom	*adresse*	*quand*	*où*	} ?
Name	Address	When	Where	

Friends and Relations

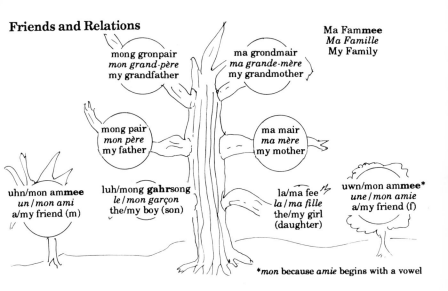

Ma Fam**mee**
Ma Famille
My Family

mong gronpair
mon grand-père
my grandfather

ma grondmair
ma grande-mère
my grandmother

mong pair
mon père
my father

ma mair
ma mère
my mother

uhn/mon am**mee**
un / mon ami
a/my friend (m)

luh/mong **gahr**song
le / mon garçon
the/my boy (son)

la/ma fee
la / ma fille
the/my girl
(daughter)

uwn/mon am**mee***
une / mon amie
a/my friend (f)

*mon because *amie* begins with a vowel

Countries and Nationalities

Eel ay fronsay*
Il est français
He is French

Ell ay fron**sez***
Elle est française
She is French

*Nationality varies slightly according to whether you are a man (m) or a woman (f)

Doo vunnay voo?
D'où venez-vous?
Where do you come from?

Zhuh vee**ang** ...
Je viens ...
I come ...

duh longlu**htair/leerlahnd**
de l'Angleterre / de l'Irlande
from England/Ireland

duh lay**koss**
de l'Écosse
from Scotland

duw pay duh **gal**
du Pays de Galles
from Wales

duh lammay**reek**
de l'Amérique
from America

duh lohstral-**lee**
de l'Australie
from Australia

duw kanad**da**
du Canada
from Canada

duh la noo**vell** zay**lahnd**
de la Nouvelle-Zélande
from New Zealand

Zhuh swee(z) ... onglay (f. ong**lez**)
Je suis anglais (f. anglaise)
I am English
(N.B. "sweez" before a vowel)

eerlonday (f. eerlon**dez**)
irlandais (f. irlandaise)
Irish

aykossay (f. aykos**sez**)
écossais (f. écossaise)
a Scot

gallwa (f. gall**waz**)
gallois (f. galloise)
Welsh

amayree**kang** (f. amayree**ken**)
américain (f. américaine)
American

ohstral-lee**ang** (f. ohstral-lee-**en**)
australien (f. australienne)
Australian

kanaddee**ang** (f. kanaddee-**en**)
canadien (f. canadienne)
Canadian

nayoh zaylon**day** (f. **-dez**)
Néo-Zélandais(e)
a New Zealander

Around the Clock and Greetings

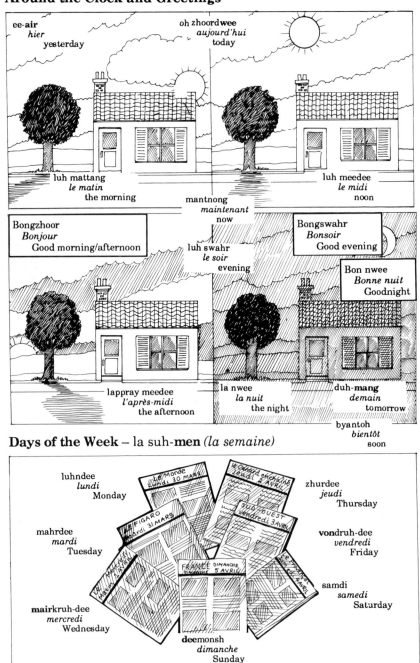

ee-**air**
hier
yesterday

oh zhoord**wee**
aujourd'hui
today

luh mattang
le matin
the morning

luh meedee
le midi
noon

mantnong
maintenant
now

Bongzhoor
Bonjour
Good morning/afternoon

luh swahr
le soir
evening

Bongswahr
Bonsoir
Good evening

Bon nwee
Bonne nuit
Goodnight

lappray meedee
l'après-midi
the afternoon

la nwee
la nuit
the night

duh-**mang**
demain
tomorrow

byantoh
bientôt
soon

Days of the Week – la suh-**men** *(la semaine)*

luhndee
lundi
Monday

zhurdee
jeudi
Thursday

mahrdee
mardi
Tuesday

vondruh-dee
vendredi
Friday

mairkruh-dee
mercredi
Wednesday

samdi
samedi
Saturday

deemonsh
dimanche
Sunday

70

lay sezzong	lay mwa	luh tong
les saisons	*les mois*	*le temps*
the seasons	**the months**	**the weather**

oh **prantong**	*au printemps*	in spring

marce
mars
March

meh
mai
May

eel fay duw vong
il fait du vent
it's windy

Pakk
Pâques
Easter

avreel
avril
April

eel plur
il pleut
it's raining

on aytay	*en été*	in summer

zhwang
juin
June

oo
août
August

luh sollay bree
le soleil brille
the sun shines

zhweeyay
juillet
July

eel fay shoh
il fait chaud
it's hot

on oh**tom**	*en automne*	in autumn

sept**ombr**
septembre
September

novv**ombr**
novembre
November

luh veen**yobl**
le vignoble
wine-picking

ok**tobbr**
octobre
October

eel fay frwa
il fait froid
it's cold

on eevair	*en hiver*	in winter

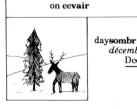

day**sombr**
décembre
December

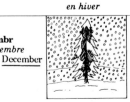

fayvreeay
février
February

Noh-**ell**
Nöel
Christmas

zhonveeay
janvier
January

eel nezh
il neige
it's snowing

Time

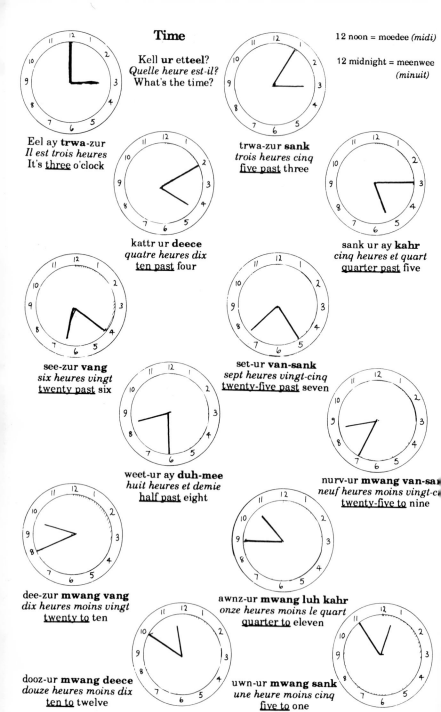

Kell ur etteel?
Quelle heure est-il?
What's the time?

12 noon = moedee *(midi)*

12 midnight = meenwee
(minuit)

Eel ay **trwa**-zur
Il est trois heures
It's <u>three</u> o'clock

trwa-zur **sank**
trois heures cinq
<u>five past</u> three

kattr ur **deece**
quatre heures dix
<u>ten past</u> four

sank ur ay **kahr**
cinq heures et quart
<u>quarter past</u> five

see-zur **vang**
six heures vingt
<u>twenty past</u> six

set-ur **van-sank**
sept heures vingt-cinq
<u>twenty-five past</u> seven

weet-ur ay **duh-mee**
huit heures et demie
<u>half past</u> eight

nurv-ur **mwang van-sank**
neuf heures moins vingt-c
<u>twenty-five to</u> nine

dee-zur **mwang vang**
dix heures moins vingt
<u>twenty to</u> ten

awnz-ur **mwang luh kahr**
onze heures moins le quart
<u>quarter to</u> eleven

dooz-ur **mwang deece**
douze heures moins dix
<u>ten to</u> twelve

uwn-ur **mwang sank**
une heure moins cinq
<u>five to</u> one

Booking Accommodation

Madame / Monsieur, — Dear Sir or Madam,

Hotels: *Je voudrais réserver une / deux chambre(s)* simple(s) / double(s)* (avec salle de bain / douche) pour — nuit(s) du — au —.*
I should like to book one/two single/double room(s) (with bath/shower) for — night(s) from — to —.
A combien s'élèvent les arrhes pour la réservation (de la / des*) chambre(s)*?
How much deposit is required to book the room(s)?

Camping: *Je voudrais réserver un emplacement (à l'ombre) (avec branchement électrique) dans votre terrain de camping.*
I should like to book a pitch (in the shade) (with electricity) on your campsite.
Je souhaiterais rester — nuit(s)* du — au —.
I wish to stay — night(s) from — to —.

Nous possédons une voiture / une caravane / un camping-car et une grande / petite tente (avec auvent).
We have a car/caravan/motor caravan and a large/small tent (with awning).
A combien s'élèvent les arrhes pour la réservation de l'emplacement?
How much deposit is required to book the pitch?

Nous serons — adulte(s)* et — enfant(s)* âgé(s) de — an(s)*.
Our party consists of — adult(s) and — child(ren) aged —.
Veuillez me communiquer vos tarifs.
Please let me know what your rates are.

Je vous prie d'agréer l'expression de mes salutations distingués,
Yours faithfully,

*add "s" if more than one.

Potted Grammar
or How French Works

Nouns are names of things, people or places. In French all nouns are thought of as either masculine (m.) or feminine (f.).

When talking about one thing only, i.e. **singular** (s.), **A** is *un* (m.) or *une* (f.) e.g.:
 un billet (a ticket), *une chambre* (a room).

If there is more than one, i.e. **plural** (pl.), use *des* in all cases, e.g.:
 des billets (some tickets), *des chambres* (some rooms).

The (singular) is *le* (m.): *le billet* (the ticket)
      la (f.): *la chambre* (the room)
  l' in front of a vowel: *l'auto* (the car)

If the noun is plural, use *les* in all cases:
 les billets (the tickets), *les chambres* (the rooms), *les autos* (the cars).
Most nouns add an s in the plural but it is not pronounced.

Adjectives describe nouns. If a noun is masculine the adjective describing it will be too. If the noun is feminine or if there is more than one, the adjective will change accordingly, but these changes are not always noticeable in the spoken language, e.g.:
 un mouchoir blanc (a white handkerchief)
 une fleur blanche (a white flower)
Adjectives may come before or after the noun.

This/that is *ce* before masculine nouns
     cet before masculine vowels or silent h
    cette before feminine nouns
These/those is *ces* in all cases.

Possessive adjectives
 The word used for "my", "your", etc. depends on whether the **following** word is masculine, feminine or plural, e.g.:
 mon billet (my ticket), *ma fleur* (my flower), *mes autos* (my cars)

	(m)	(f)	(pl)		(m)	(f)	(pl)
my	*mon*	*ma*	*mes*	our	*notre*	*notre*	*nos*
your (s.)	*ton*	*ta*	*tes*	your (pl.)	*votre*	*votre*	*vos*
his, hers, its	*son*	*sa*	*ses*	their	*leur*	*leur*	*leurs*

There is no difference between his, hers or its, e.g.:
 son fils means *his* or *her* son
 sa maison means *his* or *her* house
 ses chambres means *his, her* or *its* rooms

Pronouns are people or things:

	je	we	*nous*
you (s.)	*tu*	you (pl.)	*vous*
he, it (m.)	*il*	they (m.)	*ils*
he, it (f.)	*elle*	they (f.)	*elles*

The word used for "it" or "they" depends on whether the noun concerned is masculine or feminine, e.g.:

la chambre est grande (the room is big)
elle est grande (it is big)

tu is used only with children and close friends. As a rule you should use *vous* whether talking to one person or several.

Verbs: Endings vary according to who is doing the action:

to be	*être*	to speak	*parler*
I am	*je suis*	I speak	*je parle*
you are	*tu es)*	(you speak	*tu parles)*
he/she/it is	*il / elle est*	he/she/it speaks	*il / elle parle*
we are	*nous sommes*	we speak	*nous parlons*
you are	*vous êtes*	you speak	*vous parlez*
they are	*ils / elles sont*	they speak	*ils / elles parlent*

to have	*avoir*	to come	*venir*
I have	*j'ai*	I come	*je viens*
you have	*tu as)*	(you come	*tu viens)*
he/she/it has	*il / elle a*	he/she/it comes	*il / elle vient*
we have	*nous avons*	we come	*nous venons*
you have	*vous avez*	you come	*vous venez*
they have	*ils / elles ont*	they come	*ils / elles viennent*

to go	*aller*	to be able	*pouvoir*
I go	*je vais*	I can	*je peux*
you go	*tu vas)*	(you can	*tu peux)*
he/she/it goes	*il / elle va*	he/she/it can	*il / elle peut*
we go	*nous allons*	we can	*nous pouvons*
you go	*vous allez*	you can	*vous pouvez*
they go	*ils / elles vont*	they can	*ils / elles peuvent*

Negatives: If you want to say you don't do something you need to put *ne* before the verb and *pas* after it, e.g.:

je ne parle pas français (I don't speak French)

Questions: There are two ways of asking a question. Take the basic statement *Vous parlez anglais* (You speak English) and either –
1. turn it round: *Parlez-vous anglais?* (Do you speak English?) or
2. use *est-ce que* in front of the basic statement: *Est-ce que vous parlez anglais?* (Do you speak English?)

Index

Dégustation tasting   Look for

Loss

Shower

Numbers

0 zayroh *zéro*	18 deezweet *dix-huit*	72 swassont-dooz *soixante-douze*
1 uhn, uwn *un, une*	19 deeznurf *dix-neuf*	80 kattr-vang *quatre-vingts*
2 dur *deux*	20 vang *vingt*	81 kattr-vang-uhn *quatre-vingt-un*
3 trwa *trois*	21 vantayuhn *vingt et un*	82 kattr-vang-dur *quatre-vingt-deux*
4 kattr *quatre*	22 vandur *vingt-deux*	90 kattr-vang-deece *quatre-vingt-dix*
5 sank *cinq*	23 vantrwa *vingt-trois*	91 kattr-vang-awnz *quatre-vingt-onze*
6 seece *six*	24 vankattr *vingt-quatre*	92 kattr-vang-dooz *quatre-vingt-douze*
7 set *sept*	25 vansank *vingt-cinq*	100 song *cent*
8 weet *huit*	26 vantseece *vingt-six*	101 song uhn *cent un*
9 nurf *neuf*	27 vantset *vingt-sept*	102 song dur *cent deux*
10 deece *dix*	28 vantweet *vingt-huit*	150 song sangkont *cent cinquante*
11 awnz *onze*	29 vantnurf *vingt-neuf*	500 sank song *cinq cents*
12 dooz *douze*	30 tront *trente*	1000 meel *mille*
13 trez *treize*	40 karront *quarante*	1200 meel duh song *mille deux cents*
14 kattorz *quatorze*	50 sangkont *cinquante*	
15 kanz *quinze*	60 swassont *soixante*	1st prumyay *premier*
16 sez *seize*	70 swassont-deece *soixante-dix*	2nd duh-zyem *deuxième*
17 dee-set *dix-sept*	71 swassont ay awnz *soixante et onze*	3rd trwa-zyem troisième